World Book, Inc.
233 N. Michigan Ave.
Chicago, IL 60601 U.S.A.

For information about other World Book publications, visit our Web site at **http://www.worldbook.com** or call **1-800-WORLDBK (967-5325)**. For information about sales to schools and libraries, call **1-800-975-3250 (United States); 1-800-837-5365 (Canada)**.

World Book, Inc.
Editor in Chief: Paul A. Kobasa
Managing Editor: Maureen Mostyn Liebenson
Graphics and Design Manager: Sandra M. Dyrlund
Research Services Manager: Loranne K. Shields
Permissions Editor: Janet T. Peterson

Library of Congress Cataloging-in-Publication Data
The respiratory system.
    p. cm. -- (World Book's human body works)
  Includes bibliographical references and index.
  ISBN-13: 978-0-7166-4428-6
  ISBN-10: 0-7166-4428-2
  1. Respiratory organs--Juvenile literature. I. World Book, Inc.
II. Series.
QP121.R466 2007
612.2--dc22
                        2006004691

World Book's Human Body Works (set)
ISBN 13: 978-0-7166-4425-5
ISBN 10: 0-7166-4425-8

Printed in China

07 08 09 10 5 4 3 2

Product development: Arcturus Publishing Limited
Writer: Andrew Solway
Editor: Alex Woolf
Designer: Jane Hawkins

Acknowledgments
Corbis: cover and 15 (Jose Luis Pelaez, Inc.), 4 (Grace/Zefa), 5 (Stephen Frink), 7 (Tom and Dee Ann McCarthy), 13 (Michael A. Keller/Zefa), 17 (Jose Luis Pelaez, Inc.), 20 (Reuters/Jorge Silva), 23 (James L. Amos), 24 (David Turnley), 27 (Viviane Moos), 37 (Craig Aurness), 38 (Reuters/Denis Balibouse), 40 (Howard Davies), 41 (George Hall), 42 (Jeffrey L. Rotman), 44 (Rob Lewine).
Michael Courtney: 6, 11, 12, 16, 22, 26, 33.
Rex Features: 21 (Edward Garner), 39 (Franck Faugere).
Science Photo Library: 8 (John Bavosi), 9 (Eye of Science), 10 (Innerspace Imaging), 14 (Zephyr), 18 (Matt Meadows, Peter Arnold, Inc.), 19 (NIBSC), 25 (NASA), 28 (Dr Philippa Uwins, Whistler Research Pty), 29 (Kenneth Eward/Biografx), 30 (Andrew Lambert Photography), 31 (Dr Jeremy Burgess), 32 (BSIP, Sercomi), 34 (NIBSC), 35 (SIU, Peter Arnold, Inc.), 36 (Damien Lovegrove), 43 (Alexis Rosenfeld), 45 (Robert Brook).

Note: The content of this book does not constitute medical advice. Consult appropriate health-care professionals in matters of personal health, medical care, and fitness.

Features included in this book:

- **FAQs** Each spread contains an FAQ panel. FAQ stands for Frequently Asked Question. The panels contain answers to typical questions that relate to the topic of the spread.

- **Glossary** There is a glossary of terms on pages 46–47. Terms defined in the glossary are *italicized* on their first appearance on any spread.

- **Additional resources** Books for further reading and recommended Web sites are listed on page 47. Because of the nature of the Internet, some Web site addresses may have changed since publication. The publisher has no responsibility for any such changes nor for the content of cited resources.

Contents

In, out, in, out…

Breathe in, breathe out, breathe in, breathe out. . . . Every day, for our whole life, we have to keep breathing. Why do we need to breathe all the time? What is it that we need from air?

Respiration

Respiration is another word for breathing. The human respiratory system is the lungs and all the other body parts we use to breathe. We breathe because our body needs a *gas* called *oxygen* from the air. When we breathe, we also get rid of the gas *carbon dioxide*, which the body produces as waste. In this book you can find out exactly how the respiratory system works and how oxygen gets into and carbon dioxide gets out of the body.

Inside the cells

What happens to oxygen once it gets into the body? What exactly is it used for? The human body is made up of billions of tiny structures called *cells*. Oxygen is needed by every one of these cells for a process called cellular respiration. Find out what cellular respiration is for and how it works on pages 30 and 31.

When we breathe out, we get rid of the gas carbon dioxide from our lungs.

What else breathes?

Humans are not the only living things that breathe air to obtain oxygen. Other land animals need to breathe, too. Fish and other water creatures get oxygen directly from water. Even *bacteria* and other *microbes* need oxygen, although a few microbes can live without it. Nearly every living thing on earth needs to breathe. Plants take in carbon dioxide to make their food. In the process of making food, plants create oxygen, which is given off into the air for us to breathe.

Not only for oxygen

Breathing is important for reasons other than getting oxygen. We use our breath to talk, sing, laugh, and whistle. A part of the respiratory system called the *larynx* uses breath to make sounds. You can find out what the larynx looks like and how it works on pages 22 and 23.

FAQ

Q. How many breaths do we take in a lifetime?

A. We take about 900 breaths every hour of our life. Over a lifetime of 70 years, that is over 550 million breaths!

Like all fish, this shark gets oxygen directly from water. Water passes in through the shark's mouth, over the gills and out through the gill slits (visible here behind its head). The gills draw dissolved oxygen out of the water and into the shark's blood.

The respiratory system

Breathing is also known as respiration. The mouth, nose, pharynx (upper throat), *larynx* (voice box), *trachea* (windpipe) and a pair of lungs together make up the respiratory system. However, other parts of the body are also essential to breathing. The rib cage is involved in breathing movements. So is the *diaphragm*, a large muscle that divides the chest from the *abdomen*. Breathing is an automatic body function, controlled by our nervous system.

What happens when we breathe?

When we breathe in, or inhale, the chest expands (gets larger). This draws air into the lungs through the nose or sometimes the mouth. Inside the lungs, some of the *oxygen* from the air is released into the blood. At the same time, *carbon dioxide* from the blood is released into the lungs.

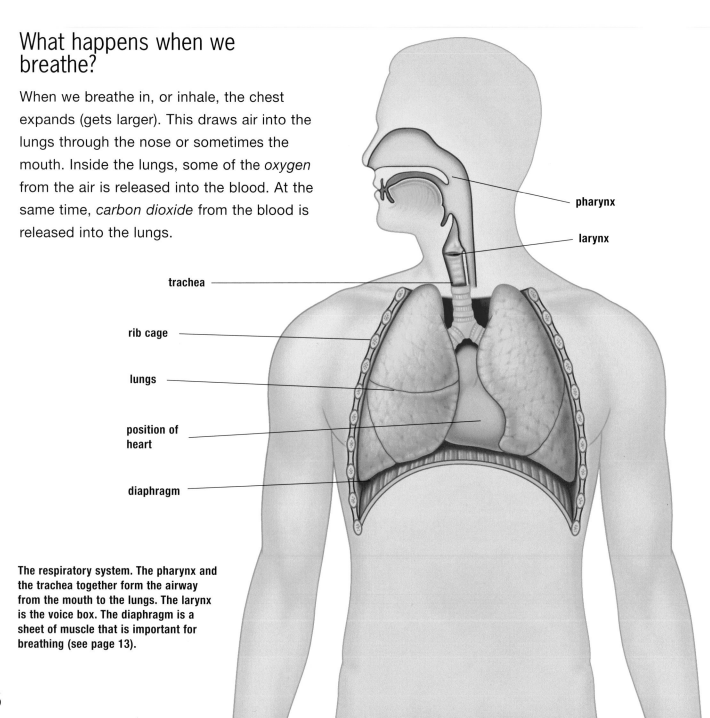

pharynx

larynx

trachea

rib cage

lungs

position of heart

diaphragm

The respiratory system. The pharynx and the trachea together form the airway from the mouth to the lungs. The larynx is the voice box. The diaphragm is a sheet of muscle that is important for breathing (see page 13).

When you breathe out, or exhale, the chest contracts (gets smaller), and this pushes air full of carbon dioxide out of the lungs. Once the exhalation, or expiration, has finished, you inhale again.

Lung capacity

At rest, about 30 cubic inches (0.5 liter) of air passes in and out of the lungs with each breath. However, our lungs hold a lot more air than this. If an average adult breathes in as much air as possible, then breathes out as much as possible, he or she will breathe out about 287 cubic inches (4.7 liters) of air. This amount is known as the vital capacity of the lungs.

Even at the end of your deepest breath, there are about 73 cubic inches (1.2 liters) of air in the lungs. This residual air cannot be removed. Together with the vital capacity, this makes a total lung capacity of 360 cubic inches (5.9 liters).

FAQ

Q. Can lung capacity change?

A. An average adult has a vital capacity of about 287 cubic inches (4.7 liters). However, exercise, especially endurance exercise, can increase the vital capacity of the lungs. Top endurance athletes can have a vital capacity of up to about 397 cubic inches (6.5 liters). Lung disease and smoking, on the other hand, both decrease the vital capacity of the lungs.

If you take a deep breath, then blow into a balloon until you cannot blow any more, you will get a good idea of how much air your lungs can hold.

Nose and throat

Most of the time you breathe in and out through your nose. The nose is not just a simple tube leading to the lungs. A lot happens to the air as it travels through the nasal passages.

Structure of the nose

The outside part of the nose is made up of two nostrils divided by a wall of tough but springy material called cartilage. Inside the head, each nostril leads to a broad nasal passage that narrows at the back to a tube called the *nasopharynx*. Three shelflike bony structures, known as turbinates or conchae, stick out from the walls of the nasal passages. The turbinates make the air swirl around as it passes through the nose. The inner surfaces of the nose and the turbinates are covered in very fine hairs called *cilia*. The surface of the nasal passages is coated with sticky *mucus*.

Air filter

The air coming into the body is changed in several ways as it travels through the nose. As the air swirls around, it is warmed and moistened. The nose also acts as a filter. Dust and other particles in the air stick to the mucus on the surface of the nasal passages.

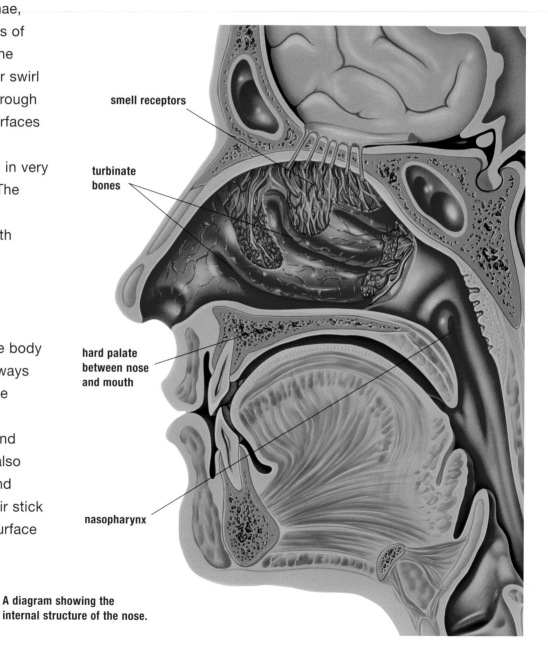

smell receptors

turbinate bones

hard palate between nose and mouth

nasopharynx

A diagram showing the internal structure of the nose.

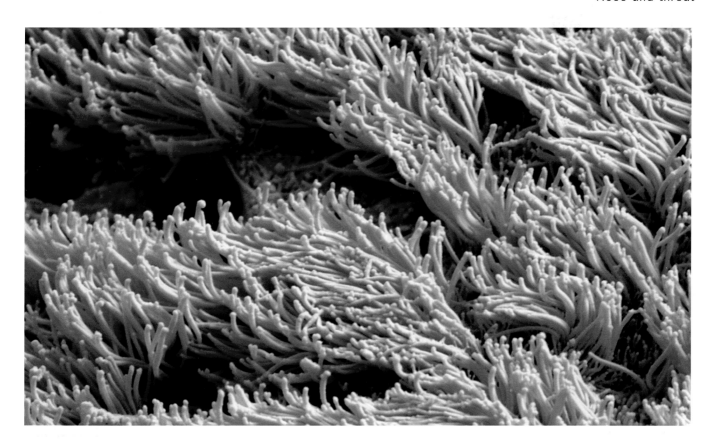

The cilia on the nose lining wave back and forth, creating a flow of mucus out of the nose and into the throat, where the mucus is swallowed.

Some of the particles coming into the nose are *bacteria* and other *microbes*. Most of these microbes are harmless, but a few can cause infections and disease. To prevent this from happening, the mucus in the nose contains special *cells* that can destroy dangerous microbes.

Sense of smell

As air passes through the nose, we smell any odors it carries. A patch of *tissue* at the very top of the nose is sensitive to the smell of chemicals in the air we breathe in. Nerve endings in this tissue are called olfactory nerve receptors. They send messages to the brain. The brain translates the messages into what we experience as smells. Our nose contains millions of smell receptor cells.

A magnified view of the lining of the nose, showing the cilia that trap and get rid of particles from the air.

FAQ

Q. Why does your nose block up when you cry?

A. The lacrimal (tear) duct in the corner of each eye has a tube connecting to the nasal passages. When you cry, some of the overflow from the tear ducts goes down this tube and floods the nose.

Looking at the lungs

A pair of lungs takes up most of the space in the chest. The other major organ in the chest is the heart. Each lung is a complex network of air passages, like a tree with millions of branches.

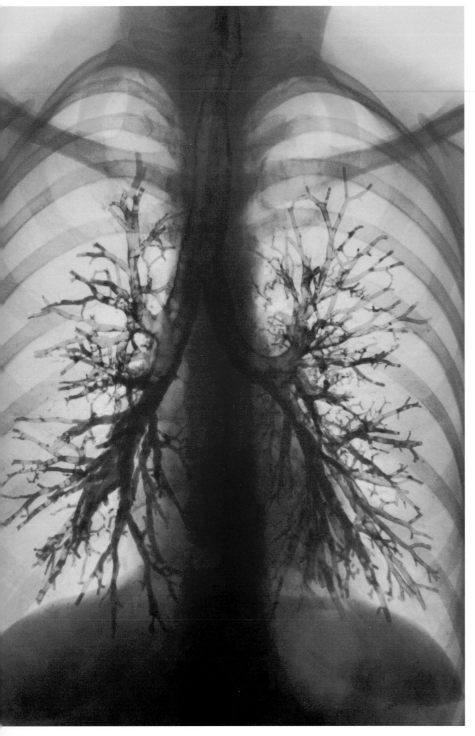

From nose to lungs

From the nose, air goes down the *trachea*, or windpipe. The trachea begins at the back of the mouth. It is a large tube that runs down the neck into the upper chest. The trachea splits into two *bronchi*, one going to the left lung and one to the right.

The esophagus, or food pipe, also starts at the back of the mouth. To keep pieces of food from getting into the lungs, we stop breathing when we swallow, and a flap of *tissue* called the epiglottis closes over the opening of the trachea. Just below the epiglottis is the *larynx*, or voice box.

A branching tree

Inside each lung, the bronchi divide into two smaller tubes called *bronchioles*. The bronchioles then divide again and again, many times, to form millions of tiny air passages. At the end of the smallest bronchioles are microscopic, air-filled sacs called *alveoli*.

This X-ray shows some of the branching air tubes inside the lungs.

A human lung contains hundreds of millions of alveoli. This gives the lungs a huge internal surface area. Your two lungs would fit comfortably in a typical carry-on suitcase. But if you spread out the insides of a pair of lungs of average size, they would cover about a fourth to a third of a tennis court.

Blood connections

Wound in among the airways of the lungs is a network of tiny blood vessels known as *capillaries*. The capillaries bring blood into the lungs to be recharged with *oxygen* from the air. The blood comes from the heart through the pulmonary arteries. After it has been recharged with oxygen, the blood goes back to the heart through the pulmonary veins and is then pumped around the body.

This enlargement of one microscopic bronchiole shows how the airways end in tiny alveoli, richly supplied with blood.

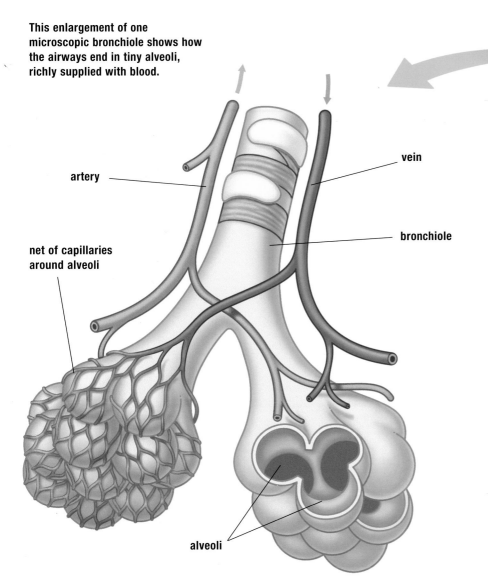

artery

vein

lung

net of capillaries around alveoli

bronchiole

alveoli

FAQ

Q. How do the lungs stay clean?

A. Although the air is cleaned in the nose before it enters the lungs, some *microbes* and particles still get into the lungs. To deal with this problem, large *white blood cells* called macrophages destroy foreign particles they encounter on the lung surfaces.

Breathing in

Breathing in is also known as *inspiration* or inhalation. When we breathe in, it is not the lungs that do the work. Muscles all around the chest work to make the chest expand, and the lungs follow.

Sticking together

The chest and the lungs move together because the outside of the lungs sticks to the inside of the chest. The outside of the lungs is covered in a smooth *membrane* called the *pleura*. Another pleural membrane covers the inside surface of the chest. Between these two membranes is only a thin layer of liquid. The two layers stick together because no air gets between them.

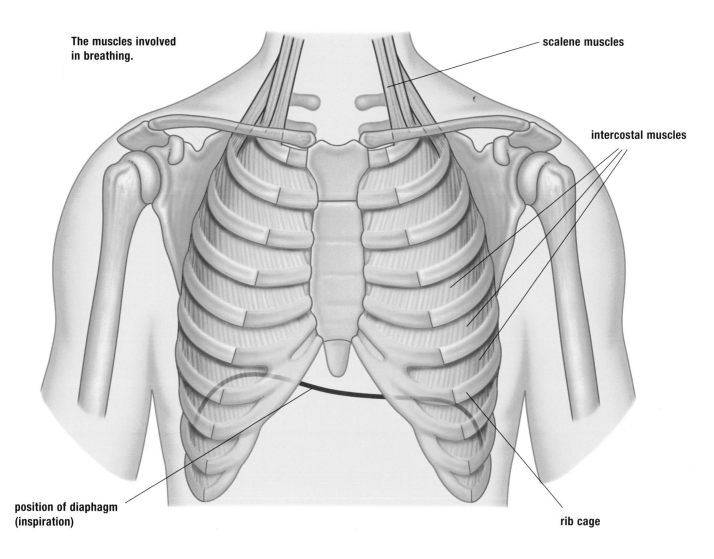

The muscles involved in breathing.

scalene muscles

intercostal muscles

position of diaphagm (inspiration)

rib cage

Inspirational muscles

The *diaphragm* is the main muscle of inspiration. It is fastened to the bottom edge of the rib cage and arches up under the lungs. When you breathe in, the muscles of the diaphragm contract and shorten. This pulls the center of the diaphragm down, making the chest deeper. More than half of the total increase in chest volume is produced by the movement of the diaphragm.

Muscles between the ribs are also involved in inspiration. The ribs slant down, and are free to move some distance up and down. When the rib muscles contract, they pull the ribs up and out.

Drawing in air

The contractions of the diaphragm and the rib muscles expand the chest, making it wider and deeper. As the chest expands, the lungs expand, too, drawing in air through the nose to fill the space in the lungs.

FAQ

Q. What is artificial respiration?

A. Someone may stop breathing because of a shock or other injury to his or her body. Artificial respiration is breathing temporarily for a person who has stopped breathing. One kind of artificial respiration is called mouth-to-mouth resuscitation. You breathe for the person by placing your mouth over his or hers and blowing air into his or her lungs, then taking your mouth away to let the air come out again. Check with your local emergency medical services agencies to learn how to give artificial respiration properly.

With practice, singers can greatly increase their maximum lung capacity.

13

Controlling respiration

Breathing gives us *oxygen*, which our bodies use to get energy. So when we need extra energy, we have to breathe more. If you run up the stairs, for example, your breathing will become deeper and faster. The body needs extra oxygen even for a few seconds of exercise.

Brain stem

The basic rhythm of breathing comes from a part of the brain called the brain stem. The brain stem has two parts, the pons (the upper part) and the medulla (the lower part). The brain stem sends out regular messages in the form of electrical impulses through nerves to the muscles of the *diaphragm* and chest wall, stimulating the muscles to contract. When this happens, you breathe in. The brain stem then sends a second set of messages stopping the first messages. The muscles relax, and you breathe out. These two sets of messages together control the breathing rhythm.

brain   brain stem

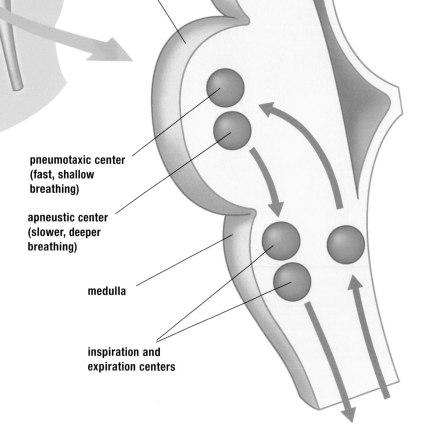

pons

pneumotaxic center
(fast, shallow
breathing)

apneustic center
(slower, deeper
breathing)

medulla

inspiration and
expiration centers

The inspiration center, right, in the medulla is the main center controlling normal breathing. It is active during inspiration and quiet during expiration. The expiration center is only active during exercise, when you need to forcibly breathe out.

Changes to the rhythm

The control of breathing is complex because many things can influence it. Your conscious brain can change your breathing; for example, if you decide to hold your breath for a short time. There also are many changes to your breathing rhythm that happen unconsciously. For example, low levels of oxygen in the blood stimulate the body to breathe faster.

However, the most important influence on breathing rhythm is the level of the *gas carbon dioxide* in your blood. The body needs to get rid of carbon dioxide because if it builds up in the body *tissues*, it makes them more acidic. This is bad for the body and can prevent it from working properly.

For this reason, the body is very sensitive to carbon dioxide. Special cells in the blood and brain pick up any changes in carbon dioxide levels in the body. If carbon dioxide levels increase dangerously, the brain stem changes the rhythm of breathing, causing you to breathe faster and more deeply, inhaling more oxygen and exhaling more carbon dioxide. As a result, the levels of carbon dioxide in the blood fall, and your breathing gradually returns to normal.

FAQ

Q. Why do we yawn?

A. When we are tired or perhaps bored, we may yawn, opening our mouth wide and drawing in a deep breath. We may also stretch our arms or other parts of the body as we yawn. Yawning happens when the body is relaxed and inactive. The purpose may be to get more oxygen into the body and stimulate it to become active.

During heavy exercise, carbon dioxide levels in the blood increase and our breathing becomes deeper and faster. We carry on breathing deeply for a short while after exercise because it takes time for carbon dioxide levels to get back to normal.

Lung defenses

Wherever our bodies connect with the outside world, we need defenses to help avoid injury or to prevent infection by microscopic germs.

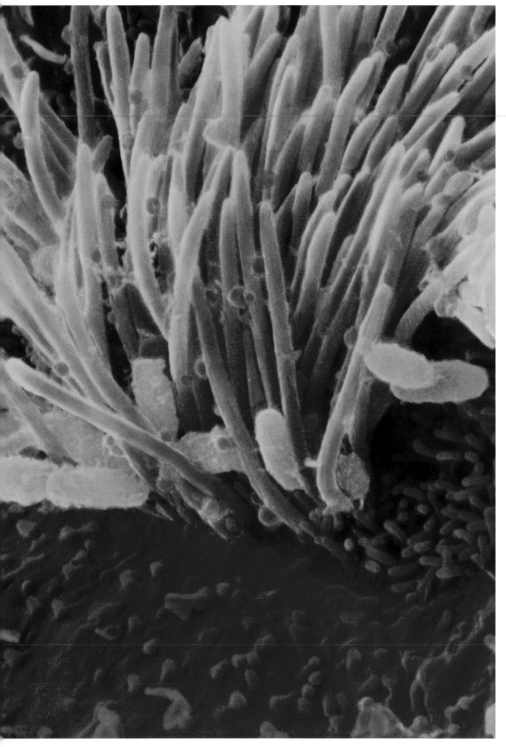

Sticky membranes

The inside of the nose and tubes leading to the lungs are covered with tiny hairs and sticky *mucus*. These surfaces help in cleaning the air breathed in through the nose (see page 9). Inside the lungs the *cilia* (hairs) all move back and forth in the same rhythm, gradually pushing any particles trapped in the mucus up and out of the *trachea*. The mucus that is then swallowed moves safely into the stomach.

Coughing and sneezing

Coughs and sneezes are some of the body's responses to attacks on the respiratory system. We start coughing or sneezing if something is irritating our nose or throat. When we cough, our stomach and *diaphragm* muscles contract suddenly, sending a high-speed jet of air up our throat and out of our mouth.

In this magnified view of the trachea, the yellow ovals are bacteria that cause whooping cough.

We sneeze when the nose lining is irritated. The sneeze shoots a cloud of mucus and other particles out of the nose. A person should cover his or her nose and mouth when he or she coughs or sneezes.

A few coughs usually will clear out any particles in the airways. A sneeze is similar to a cough, but the air goes out through the nose rather than through the mouth.

Hiccups

Hiccups do not have a purpose in the same way as coughs and sneezes. A hiccup is a sudden spasm in the diaphragm that makes you draw in air with a funny yelping noise. Hiccups can be caused by eating or drinking too much. An attack of hiccups usually lasts only a few minutes, but it can go on for hours or even days. You can sometimes stop hiccups by breathing deeply, briefly holding your breath, or breathing rapidly into a paper bag.

FAQ

Q. What is an allergy?

A. When some people are outside in the summertime, their nose and eyes start to run and the people sneeze repeatedly. Other people can have similar problems in a house where there are dogs or cats. These are examples of people with *allergies*. An allergy is a body reaction that occurs in a person who is sensitive to a certain substance, such as plant pollen or pet hair. The sensitivity can cause sneezing and other symptoms.

Breathing faster and slower

When we exercise, we breathe faster and sometimes get "out of breath." When we rest, our breathing slows down and becomes shallower. These changes show that we need *oxygen* whenever we are using energy.

Exercise

The most obvious changes to breathing happen during exercise or other strenuous activity. Soon after we begin exercising, we will begin to breathe faster and more deeply. If we continue to exercise vigorously, we will soon begin to feel out of breath. This happens because our respiratory and *circulatory* systems cannot keep up with the energy demands of our muscles. The muscles are not getting enough oxygen, and they are producing more *carbon dioxide* waste than the body can get rid of. Very soon we have to stop and rest and "catch our breath."

If the exercise we do is less vigorous and more evenly paced—for example, cycling or swimming at an average pace—at first our breathing will get

When we cycle fast, we must breathe more quickly and more heavily to cope with the increased work of the muscles.

heavier and faster and we may feel out of breath. This happens because our body takes a little time to adjust to the higher levels of energy we are using. However, after a while our breathing usually should settle into a new rhythm and enable us to keep going at the same pace.

Sleeping

When we sleep, our breathing becomes slow and shallow. We are using very little energy, but the rate of breathing actually falls below what the body needs. As a result, when we are asleep, levels of carbon dioxide in the blood rise slightly, and oxygen levels drop. If the oxygen levels fall too low, our body reacts to wake us up to take deep breaths, or perhaps yawn.

FAQ

Q. How much oxygen do we use when we exercise?

A. We use oxygen whenever we use energy. The more energy we use, the more oxygen we need. Scientists studying exercise and sports measure the maximum amount of oxygen a person uses when he or she is exercising. They call this measurement the VO_2 max. An average adult has a VO_2 max of about 35. Top endurance athletes have a VO_2 max of 80 or more. They can take in more than twice as much oxygen per minute as the average adult.

We use little energy when we are sleeping, so our breathing becomes slow and shallow.

Making noises

Other activities related to breathing are speaking and singing. When we speak or sing, we do so on a controlled *expiration*.

Making sounds

The *larynx*, or voice box, is at the top of the *trachea*. If you feel the middle of your throat, you should be able to feel the firm material called cartilage that forms the front of the larynx. The larynx is a boxlike structure made of cartilage. Inside this box, stretched across the airway, are two vocal cords.

In normal breathing the vocal cords are relaxed and air can move easily through the trachea. When a person talks or makes other noises, muscles stretch the vocal cords and the gap between them is reduced to a thin slit. As air passes through this slit, it makes the vocal cords vibrate, and this produces sound.

When the vocal cords are tight, air passing through them causes sound vibrations. In normal breathing the vocal cords are relaxed, so they make no sound.

Changing the tone

The muscles that close and open the vocal cords can also change the amount of stretch in the vocal cords when they are closed. If the vocal cords are pulled very tight, they produce high notes; when they are looser they produce lower notes.

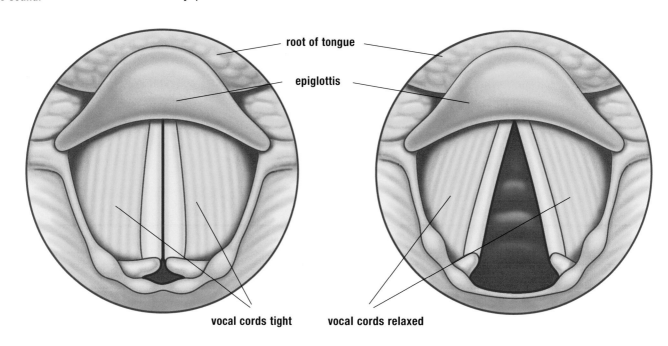

root of tongue

epiglottis

vocal cords tight   vocal cords relaxed

FAQ

Q. What is the loudest sound anyone has made?

A. The loudest human sound officially recorded was in London, England, in 2000. Jill Drake screamed at a Halloween party and her sound measured at 129 decibels. That is louder than the sound heard in the front row of a typical rock concert! A decibel is a unit used to measure sound levels. Normal conversation reaches about 60 decibels.

The mouthpiece of a clarinet includes a reed, a thin piece of cane, or woody plant stem. When a musician blows into the clarinet mouthpiece, the passing air makes the reed vibrate. The vibration makes sound in a way similar to vibrating vocal cords.

High and low sounds and a range of different noises can result from air passing through the vocal cords. However, speech involves using the mouth, tongue, and teeth to shape the sounds. You can hear how important the mouth is in shaping words by trying to speak with your mouth wide open. It is almost impossible to be understood if you talk this way.

Male and female voices

Young boys and girls have very similar, high-pitched voices. However, during puberty (the time when people mature sexually), boys' larynxes grow larger than those of girls. By the time they are adults, men's vocal cords measure about three-fourths of an inch (7.6 centimeters). The longer vocal cords make men's voices generally deeper than women's.

Absorbing area

The purpose of the respiratory system is to exchange *gas*—to exchange *carbon dioxide* for *oxygen*.

Breathe in, breathe out

In the few seconds it takes us to breathe in and breathe out again, the body gets as much oxygen as it can from the air and gets rid of as much carbon dioxide as possible. The huge surface area of the inside of the lungs helps this exchange of gases happen quickly.

You can see why a large surface area is needed if you imagine trying to mop up a pool of water on the floor. If you use a single tissue, which has only a small surface area for absorbing liquid, the job will take a very

In a spacecraft, the carbon dioxide that the astronauts breathe out is removed by filters. This makes the air supply last much longer.

long time. However, if you use a large, thick towel, which has a much larger surface area, it will take less time to mop up the water.

Changes in the air

What happens to air while it is in the lungs? How is the air breathed into the lungs different from the air breathed out? One noticeable difference is that the air coming out of the lungs is warmer and moister than the air going in.

However, the most important difference between inhaled and exhaled air is that the air you breathe out has less oxygen and more carbon dioxide in it than the air you breathe in. The air around us contains about 21 percent oxygen and a tiny amount of carbon dioxide (about 0.03 percent). In the air leaving the lungs there is only about 15 percent oxygen, and carbon dioxide levels have risen to about 5 percent.

FAQ

Q. What happens to all the carbon dioxide?

A. Billions of people and animals all around the world are constantly breathing out carbon dioxide. This carbon dioxide is then removed from the air, and oxygen is released back into the air, by green plants in a process called photosynthesis. In photosynthesis, plants combine carbon dioxide with water from the soil to make sugars, which they can use as food. As the plants burn the food for energy, they give off oxygen. The cycle of respiration and photosynthesis maintains Earth's natural balance of carbon dioxide and oxygen.

When we breathe out on a cold day, water vapor in our breath condenses (turns from gas to liquid) in the air, forming tiny droplets that look like steam.

Gas exchange

The places where *gas* exchange takes place—known as the respiratory surfaces—are the *alveoli* and the *capillaries* (tiny blood vessels) that surround them. The walls of the alveoli and the capillaries are very thin, so it is easy for gases to pass through them.

Each blood capillary is very narrow, but there are billions of them, so the amount of blood passing through the lungs at any one time is very large. At rest, the heart pumps 244 to 366 cubic inches (3.9 to 5.9 liters) of blood through the lungs every minute—almost the entire amount of blood in the body. During vigorous exercise this may rise by as much as five times to around 1,525 cubic inches (24.4 liters) per minute.

Gas exchange in the alveoli.

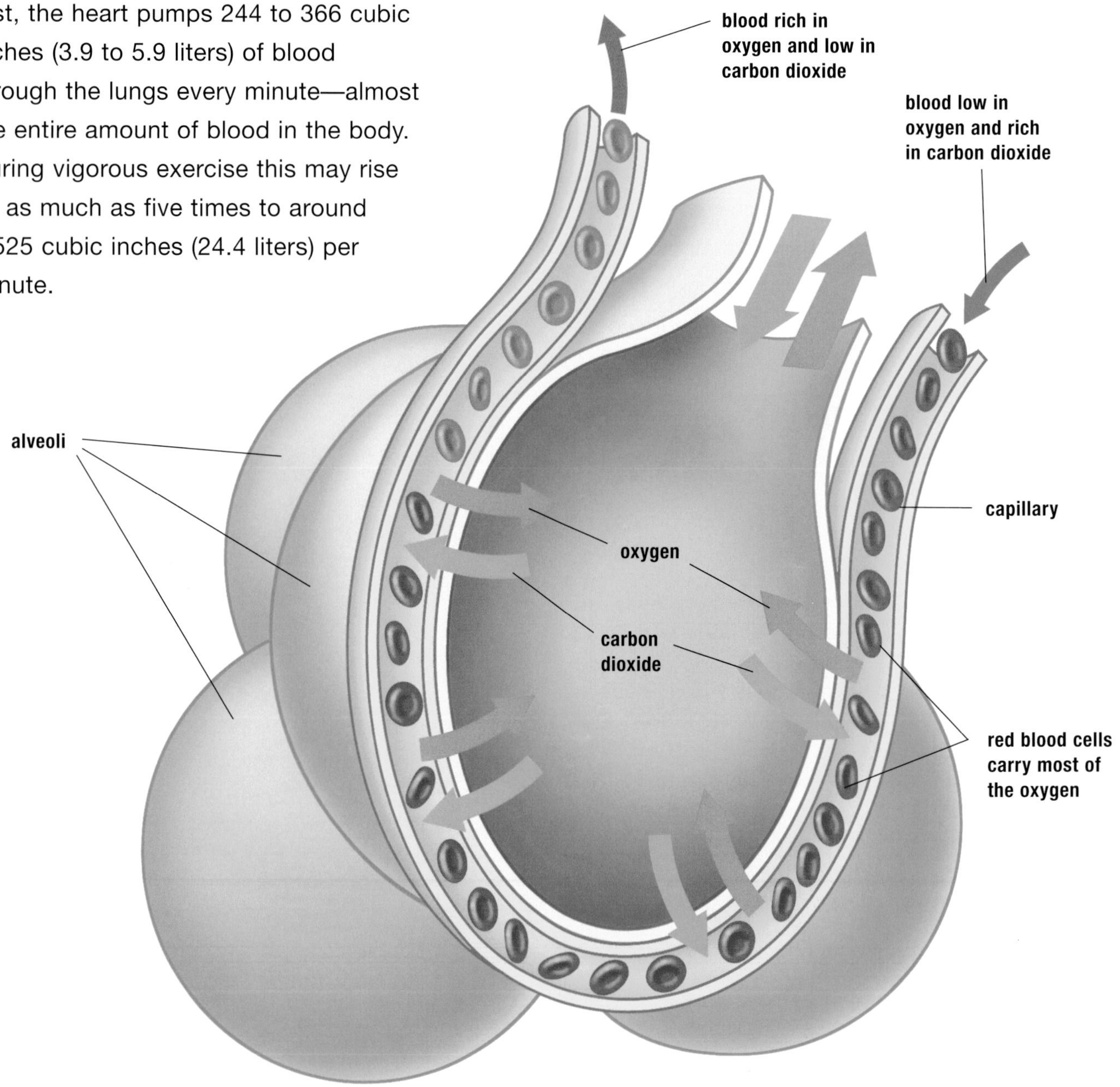

blood rich in oxygen and low in carbon dioxide

blood low in oxygen and rich in carbon dioxide

alveoli

capillary

oxygen

carbon dioxide

red blood cells carry most of the oxygen

Firefighters are equipped with oxygen tanks and masks to allow them to breathe in smoky environments.

Oxygen passes into the blood

The blood coming into the lungs has been all around the body and has given up much of its *oxygen* to the body *tissues*. As a result, the amount of oxygen in the blood is low. When we breathe in, the lungs fill up with air that is much richer in oxygen. Some of this oxygen passes out of the alveoli and into the capillaries.

Carbon dioxide passes out of the blood

The blood coming into the lungs has collected waste *carbon dioxide* from all around the body. The level of carbon dioxide in the blood is therefore high. Most of the carbon dioxide passes out of the blood and into the lungs. It then leaves the body when it is breathed out.

FAQ

Q. Can we breathe pure oxygen?

A. Oxygen is the only part of air that we really need. So perhaps breathing more oxygen would be better than breathing normal air. Some people say that breathing air enriched with oxygen gives you extra energy and makes you feel better. But most doctors do not agree. In hospitals, people with certain illnesses may be given pure oxygen for short periods to help them recover. But over the long term, too much oxygen is actually poisonous and can cause serious lung problems.

Gases in the blood

Getting *oxygen* from the lungs into the blood is a complex process. Oxygen does not dissolve easily in water or in plasma (the liquid part of blood). The blood has to have a special transportation system for collecting oxygen and carrying it around the body.

Hemoglobin

A magnified view of red blood cells in a blood vessel.

Most of your blood is made up of *red blood cells*. The red cells get their color from a substance called hemoglobin. It is hemoglobin that carries most of the oxygen in the blood.

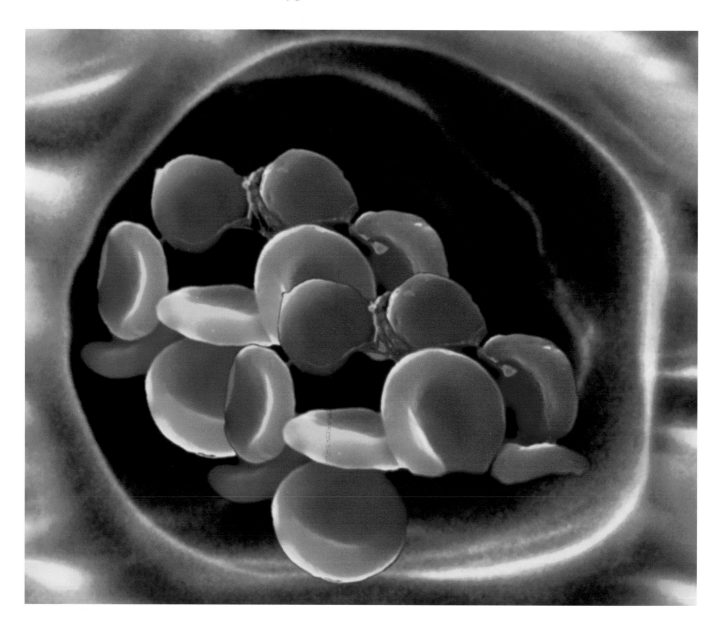

When oxygen passes from the lungs into the blood, hemoglobin *molecules* bind with oxygen molecules. This has to happen very quickly because the blood is in the lungs for only a short time. The oxygen remains bound to the hemoglobin until the blood reaches the body *tissues*. What happens next depends on whether we are at rest or active.

When we are at rest, the amount of oxygen in our tissues is quite high. At these times, hemoglobin releases only about a quarter of the oxygen it is carrying to the tissues. However, when we are active, the level of oxygen in the muscles drops much lower. When this happens, hemoglobin releases up to 90 percent of the oxygen that it is carrying.

Emergency oxygen

When muscles start to work, they need oxygen in a hurry. For this reason, muscles keep their own internal store of oxygen in the form of a *protein* called myoglobin. Myoglobin is similar to hemoglobin. Like hemoglobin, it binds oxygen, but it does so more strongly than hemoglobin. As a result, some oxygen transfers from hemoglobin in the blood to myoglobin in the muscles.

If the muscles are working hard and not getting enough oxygen, the level of oxygen in the muscles will fall very low. When this happens, the myoglobin releases its oxygen, giving the muscles an extra oxygen boost when they most need it.

FAQ

Q. How does carbon dioxide travel in the blood?

A. Most of the *carbon dioxide* in the blood is carried as bicarbonate dissolved in the plasma. A small amount (about 5 percent) is attached to hemoglobin.

This computer model shows the structure of the protein myoglobin. The red circle is an oxygen molecule bound to the myoglobin.

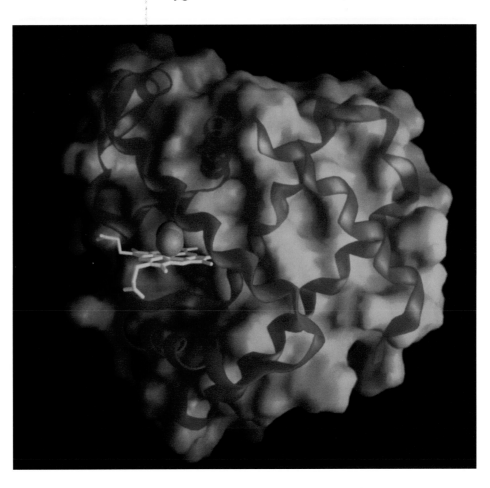

Cellular respiration

Oxygen plays an essential part in helping the body's *cells* to release energy from food. How does the body use oxygen to do this?

Producing energy

All cells, especially muscle cells, need energy to do their jobs. They get it from a substance called *ATP* (adenosine triphosphate). Cells can break down ATP to form another substance, ADP (adenosine diphosphate). The change produces energy in a form that cells can use to do their work, for example, making muscle fibers contract or sending nerve signals.

To change ATP to ADP and back again to ATP, the cell needs energy. It gets this energy from food. The main food our cells use is *glucose*, a type of sugar. Glucose is broken down to form *carbon dioxide*, water, and energy in a process called cellular respiration.

When sugar burns, oxygen combines with the sugar. The process gives off energy. Cellular respiration is a slow burning of sugar to get energy.

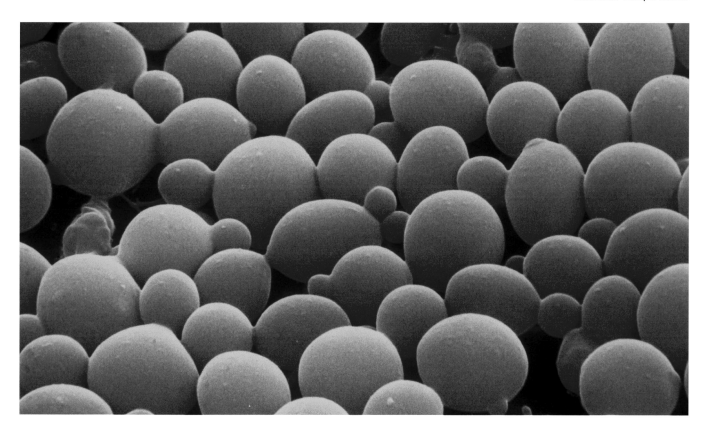

Three-stage process

Cellular respiration takes place in three stages. In the first stage glucose is broken down to form a substance called pyruvic acid. This process is called glycolysis, and it does not need oxygen. However, glycolysis produces only enough energy to make two *molecules* of ATP for each molecule of glucose broken down.

The second and third stages of cellular respiration both need oxygen. The second stage is called the Krebs cycle and it produces carbon dioxide and some ATP energy. The third stage, called oxidative phosphorylation, produces water and much more ATP energy. In total, these two stages of cellular respiration produce enough energy to make 36 molecules of ATP.

We can see from this why the body needs oxygen. Without oxygen, cells can make only two molecules of ATP from every molecule of glucose. But if oxygen is present, the cells can make 38 ATP molecules from one molecule of glucose.

Yeast cells break down sugar to produce energy in a process called fermentation, which does not require oxygen.

FAQ

Q. Do all living things need oxygen?

A. A few kinds of living things, such as yeast, can live without oxygen. They get their energy from a process called fermentation, which is similar to glycolysis. Fermentation is very inefficient because, like glycolysis, it produces only a small amount of energy.

Energy factories

If you look at muscle *cells* through a powerful microscope, the first thing you would notice are the bundles of long muscle filaments packed into the cell. Between these filaments you would see many small round or oval structures. These structures are called *mitochondria*. Mitochondria are the body's power stations. They supply cells with the energy they need to stay alive, grow, and carry out their work.

Bigger inside than out

Mitochondria are surrounded by two *membranes*—an inner and an outer skin. The outer skin is a simple covering that separates each mitochondrion from the rest of the cell. The inner membrane is wrinkled—it is bent into many tiny folds. The folds make the surface area of the inner membrane much bigger than the surface area of the outer one. This is important because many of the processes involved

This magnified section through a muscle fiber shows the many mitochondria (green) that produce the energy the muscles need to contract.

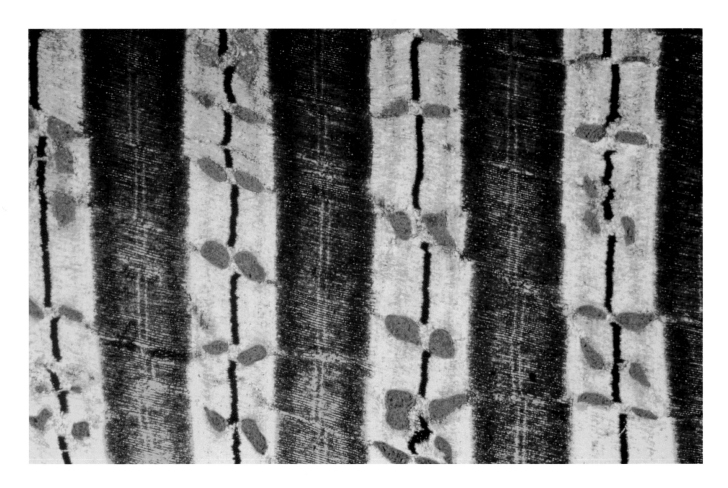

in cellular respiration happen on the surface of the inner membrane. The more wrinkled its inner surface is, the more energy the mitochondrion can produce.

Inside the power station

The stages of cellular respiration that need *oxygen* happen inside the mitochondria. The first stage, glycolysis, does not need oxygen, so this happens outside the mitochondria. The end product of glycolysis, pyruvic acid, is taken up by the mitochondria, along with oxygen. Inside the mitochondria the pyruvic acid is broken down into energy in the form of *ATP*. The mitochondria also produce water and *carbon dioxide*. The ATP, water, and carbon dioxide all pass out of the mitochondria and into the cell.

A mitochondrion takes up pyruvic acid, oxygen, and the raw materials to make ATP (ADP and phosphate) from the cell. It uses these raw materials to produce ATP, water, and carbon dioxide.

FAQ

Q. Where do mitochondria come from?

A. Scientists think that billions of years ago, mitochondria were small cells, similar to *bacteria*, that invaded larger cells and began to live inside them. Perhaps at first the invaders were parasites and killed the cells they invaded. But in time they adapted to living permanently inside the larger cells, providing them with energy in return for a regular supply of food. The invaders were the ancestors of mitochondria.

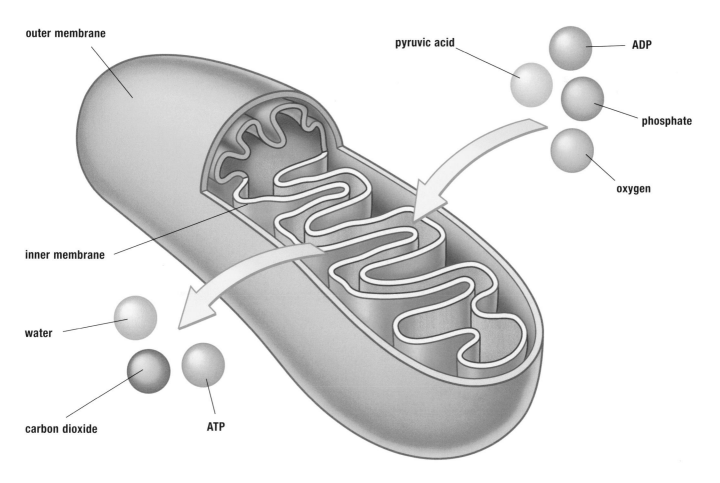

outer membrane

pyruvic acid

ADP

phosphate

oxygen

inner membrane

water

carbon dioxide

ATP

Lung problems

Most of the time our respiratory system works without problems. But sometimes things can go wrong with the respiratory system, from colds and sniffles to life-threatening diseases.

Colds and flu

A cold is a disease that affects mainly the nose and throat. The lining of these areas becomes inflamed and produces large amounts of *mucus*. The cause of these symptoms is a tiny *virus*—a germ even smaller than *bacteria*. About 200 different kinds of virus are known to cause colds.

A cold makes you feel uncomfortable for a few days, but influenza (flu) can be much worse. Flu is another disease caused by viruses, and it also affects the upper respiratory tract. The flu virus invades the *cells* of the lining of these areas and multiplies. The symptoms of flu include aching muscles, feeling tired, and a high temperature. A bout of flu will keep most people in bed for a few days. However, some strains, or types, of flu are more dangerous and can kill people.

A highly magnified view of influenza viruses on the surface of a cell.

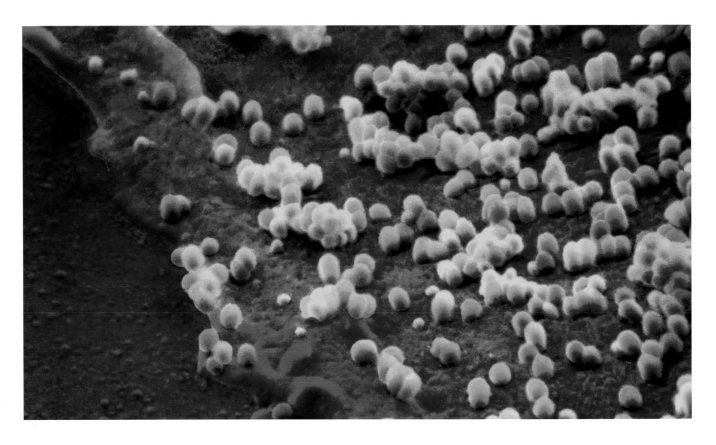

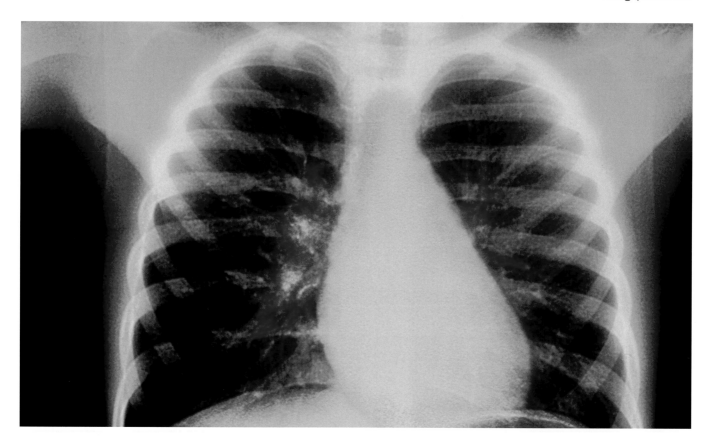

Pneumonia and tuberculosis

Pneumonia and tuberculosis (TB) are infections of the lungs. Pneumonia can be caused by many kinds of *microbes*, including fungi, but most commonly it is caused by bacteria and viruses. Pneumonia causes inflammation of the lung *tissues*. It is a severe illness that may last several weeks, but with modern antibiotics (drugs that can kill bacteria or make them inactive) most people recover.

Tuberculosis is a lung disease caused by a specific kind of bacteria called tubercle bacilli. It can cause serious damage to the lung tissues, leaving areas of scarring and dead tissue. Tuberculosis was a major cause of death around the world until the mid-1900's. Today, in countries with well-equipped hospitals and access to antibiotics, TB is no longer a major killer, but in developing countries it continues to kill many people each year.

This X-ray shows the lungs of a patient with TB. The pink areas are parts of the lung affected by TB.

FAQ

Q. Why is flu sometimes deadly?

A. Three strains of virus, known as strains A, B, and C, can cause flu. Type C flu viruses cause very mild illness in humans. Type B is the kind that usually causes local outbreaks of flu. Type A viruses can cause widespread serious illness that sometimes kills many people because the viruses can be more virulent (powerful) or people have less natural resistance to them.

Problems caused by the environment

Not all problems with the lungs are caused by *microbes*. Sometimes the way people live and work can lead to lung disorders.

Asthma

Asthma is a lung disease that can cause wheezing, coughing, and breathlessness. It has many different causes. In children it is often caused by an *allergy* (see page 19), for example, to pollen or animal hair or dander (feather, hair, and skin particles).

Many young people suffer from asthma. They often must use an inhaler to help reduce wheezing and shortness of breath.

People can suffer from asthma for many years. Some get asthma as children and then recover when they become adults. Other people first suffer from asthma as adults.

Smoking-related diseases

Scientists have found that smoking cigarettes, cigars, or pipes leads to many kinds of lung disease. The most common disease caused by smoking is lung cancer. Cancers are groups of cells that divide uncontrollably to produce growths called tumors. Lung cancer is one of the most common causes of death in developed countries.

Other lung diseases caused by smoking include bronchitis and emphysema. Bronchitis is the narrowing and inflammation of the large airways. It causes severe coughing and large amounts of *mucus*. With emphysema, groups of *alveoli* are destroyed and the lungs become less elastic. This causes serious difficulty in breathing.

The dust produced in mining and stone cutting can cause a lung disease called silicosis.

FAQ

Q. Is smoking really so bad for you?

A. In 1964, the United States surgeon general announced the first clear evidence that smoking is a cause of lung cancer. Further research has shown that smoking is linked to increased risk of other illnesses, such as heart disease, bronchitis, pneumonia, and high blood pressure. People who smoke live on average about 14 years fewer than people who do not. Since 1964, it is estimated that about 12 million Americans have died from smoking-related diseases.

Dust and pollution

Miners, stonecutters, and people who grind or polish stones for a living are all at risk of getting silicosis. This condition, caused by breathing stone dust over many years, creates scar tissue in the lungs and eventually makes them less elastic. Asbestos, a material used for building insulation, can cause a similar disease called asbestosis.

Pollution in the air also can cause lung disease. Scientists believe that the rise in the number of asthma sufferers in major cities is linked to an increase in air pollution.

Improving the lungs

Disease reduces the ability of the lungs to get *oxygen* from the air. If the body cannot get enough oxygen, it cannot get enough energy. So people with lung disease easily become tired and out of breath. In contrast, exercising regularly makes the lungs work better and the heart beat more strongly.

Anaerobic exercise

There are two basic kinds of exercise: *aerobic* (with air) and *anaerobic* (without air). All exercise is ultimately aerobic because, as you have read, the body cannot live and function without oxygen. However, for short periods of very heavy exercise, the muscles can, in fact, work without oxygen.

The first part of cellular respiration—glycolysis—does not need oxygen (see page 31), and in anaerobic exercise the muscles get energy from glycolysis alone. There is a buildup of pyruvic acid (the end product of glycolysis) in the

In the 100-meter sprint, the muscles work anaerobically. Top athletes sometimes do not breathe at all during the sprint.

muscles. Some of the pyruvic acid is turned into another substance called lactic acid, which disperses into the blood. After up to two minutes of anaerobic exercise, levels of acid build up enough that the muscles will become sluggish or will cramp.

Anaerobic exercise can happen only in short bursts because of the buildup of lactic acid. However, in those short bursts the body works to its maximum. Because of this, anaerobic exercise is good for building bigger muscles.

Exercise with air

When the muscles are not worked to their maximum, the lungs and the blood can keep them supplied with oxygen all the time. This is called aerobic exercise. In aerobic exercise the muscles do not work so hard, but they can keep working for much longer. Regular aerobic exercise makes your heart stronger and improves lung capacity.

The Tour de France is one of the most demanding endurance events in any sport. Cyclists exercise aerobically at high levels for four or five hours each day for three weeks.

FAQ

Q. How long can we keep exercising anaerobically?

A. On average, we can exercise anaerobically for up to two minutes only. But with training this can be increased. Athletes, such as sprinters, who need lots of explosive power, do short bursts of high-power exercise with long rests in between. This kind of training improves the body's ability to work anaerobically. In a 100-meter sprint race, some top athletes actually do not breathe at all.

Breathing at great heights

Some people live in mountain villages many thousands of feet or meters above sea level. But if you lived at or around sea level and you flew to one of these villages, you would probably soon feel very ill. You might have a headache, feel tired and sick, and be short of breath. All these symptoms are caused by problems with respiration at high *altitudes*.

Oxygen at height

This village in Nepal, a country in south-central Asia, is at a height of 11,614 feet (3,540 meters). At this altitude the air is less dense than at sea level, and consequently there is less oxygen.

Oxygen makes up 21 percent of the air. At sea level, this is more than enough oxygen for humans to breathe easily. However, the higher the altitude, the thinner the air—it is less dense. So, although oxygen still makes up 21 percent of the air, there is less oxygen per square foot or

meter. For instance, at the top of Mount Everest, which is 29,035 feet (8,850 meters) above sea level, there is only a fourth as much oxygen as there is at sea level.

Very few people can survive on Mount Everest without breathing equipment. But some people live at heights of about 13,000 feet (3,900 meters) above sea level, and most of us can get used to living at this height. How do people manage this?

Adapting to height

At a height of 11,500 feet (3,450 meters) the lungs get about 40 percent less oxygen per breath than at sea level. When the body first moves to this height, it adapts by taking in more air. We breathe more deeply and quickly even when at rest. If we do exercise, we would become breathless much more quickly than we would at sea level.

After a few weeks at higher altitudes the body begins to adapt. It changes in several ways in response to the thinner air. The heart pumps blood into the lung *capillaries* more strongly, and this forces blood into parts of the lungs that are not normally used. The body produces more *red blood cells* so that the blood can carry more oxygen. It also produces more of substances called phosphates, which help the release of oxygen from the red blood cells when they get to the body *tissues*.

FAQ

Q. How high can we go without breathing equipment?

A. On high mountains, climbers often use breathing equipment to give them extra oxygen. But it is possible to go without it. In 1978, mountaineers Reinhold Messner and Peter Habeler were the first people to climb Mount Everest without using extra oxygen.

Pilots flying at high altitude breathe pure oxygen.

Breathing underwater

It can be difficult for people to breathe at high *altitudes*, but it is impossible for them to breathe underwater. Fish can get *oxygen* from water through their gills, but humans and other animals with lungs cannot breathe in this way. However, it is possible to swim underwater for short periods, even without breathing equipment.

Holding your breath

Anyone who has dived into a swimming pool or swum underwater knows that we can survive underwater by holding our breath. Most people can hold their breath for half a minute or more, although it is difficult to do this when swimming underwater.

People who train to dive without using oxygen (free divers) can learn to hold their breath for a few minutes. They may be tempted to try and increase the time by overbreathing before they dive. However, overbreathing can be dangerous because the divers can end up keeping too much *carbon dioxide* in their body. As a result, they can lose consciousness while in the water.

With training it is possible to swim underwater for several minutes simply by holding the breath.

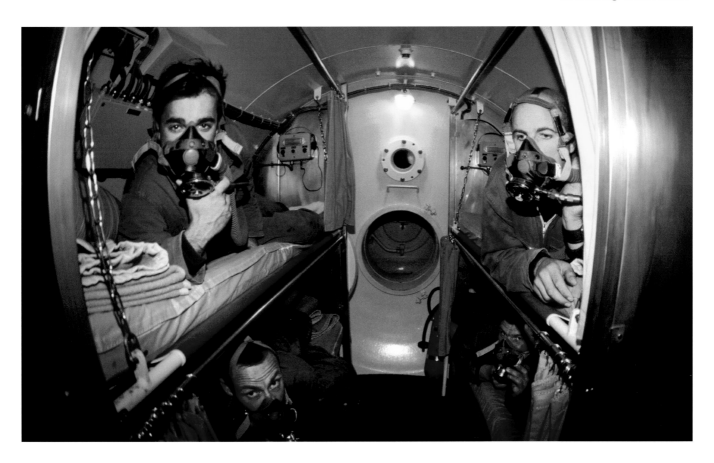

Divers at low depths for long periods often spend several hours in a decompression chamber. Doing so very gradually reduces the air pressure to prevent the divers from getting the bends.

Breathing equipment

In 1943, the aqualung was invented. This is a small cylindrical tank of air from which a diver could breathe underwater. A typical aqualung contains compressed air, or a mixture called Nitrox, which consists of about 35 percent oxygen and 65 percent *nitrogen*.

A diver cannot breathe directly from his or her tank because the force of the compressed air would damage his or her lungs. The tank is therefore fitted with a device called a regulator that reduces the pressure of the air to a level that is safe to breathe.

FAQ

Q. Are there problems with deep diving?

A. The pressure on the body in deep water can cause problems for divers. At a depth of 33 feet (10 meters) the pressure on a diver's body is twice that at the surface. This high pressure squashes the air in the lungs and pushes some of the nitrogen from this air into the blood. When the diver returns to the surface, the nitrogen is usually breathed out through the lungs. But if a diver rises too fast, bubbles of nitrogen may form in the blood. The bubbles can block blood vessels and cripple or even kill divers. This condition is known as the bends. To avoid the bends, divers must return to the surface slowly after a deep dive.

Healthy lungs

The mouth, nose, throat, and lungs make up the respiratory system. However, you have read that respiration is about much more than breathing. The heart and blood vessels play an essential role in getting *oxygen* from the lungs to the rest of the body, and every cell in the body gets energy from cellular respiration. Keeping the respiratory system healthy involves much more than just the lungs.

Regular exercise helps to keep the lungs healthy.

Keeping fit

Regular exercise throughout your life will help keep your respiratory and *circulatory* systems healthy. *Aerobic exercise* strengthens the heart and lungs and also increases blood flow to the working muscles. More blood flowing to the muscles means that the muscle *cells* get more oxygen and fuel. Exercise also increases the number of red cells in the blood, which increases the blood's oxygen-carrying capacity.

Healthy lifestyle

Smoking has been shown to cause lung cancer and many other diseases of the respiratory system, so avoiding smoking will help to keep your lungs healthy.

What you eat can also affect respiration. Eating too much and becoming overweight can put a strain on the heart, and eating foods containing too much saturated fat and cholesterol increases the risk of heart disease. Eating a balanced diet that includes these fats sparingly will help to keep the heart healthy.

Healthy environment

Polluted air that contains such substances as mining dust, car exhaust fumes, and smoke from factory chimneys can cause *allergies*, asthma, and many other kinds of lung problems. Government regulations and improvements in technology have reduced the pollutants going into the air in many countries. More can be done by private citizens; for example, by traveling by car only when strictly necessary. If we want to have healthy lungs in the future, we must all work together to reduce pollution.

There are many sources of pollution that affect the quality of the air we breathe.

FAQ

Q. Are you safe from air pollution indoors?

A. Recent research suggests that air pollution inside homes and other buildings can be worse than pollution outdoors. Tobacco smoke, stoves, heaters, and fumes given off by paints, adhesives, cleaning products, and other household chemicals are all sources of indoor air pollution. These pollutants can cause long-term health problems, such as lung and heart disease.

Glossary

abdomen The part of the body below the chest and above the pelvis containing the stomach and intestines.

aerobic exercise Exercise in which the muscles have enough oxygen to work and can keep going for long periods.

allergy An illness caused by a sensitivity to a particular substance.

altitude Height above the ground.

alveoli Tiny air sacs in the lungs.

anaerobic exercise Heavy exercise in which the muscles cannot get enough oxygen and so work for a short time without it.

ATP (adenosine triphosphate) A high-energy substance that cells can use to do work.

bacteria Very small, simple living things.

bronchi The two main air tubes that branch from the trachea.

bronchioles Small air tubes that branch from the bronchi.

capillaries Tiny blood vessels.

carbon dioxide A gas that is a waste product from cellular respiration.

cells The smallest building blocks of living things.

cilia Small hairlike projections from some cells that can wave back and forth.

circulatory system The heart and the system of blood vessels that carry blood around the body.

diaphragm The sheet of muscle that separates the chest from the abdomen.

expiration Breathing out; also called exhalation.

gas One of the three states of matter, the others being solid and liquid. Oxygen is a gas.

glucose The sugar that is the main fuel for cellular respiration.

inspiration Breathing in; also called inhalation.

larynx The voice box.

membrane A thin sheet.

microbes Microscopic living things.

mitochondria Tiny structures inside living cells where cellular respiration takes place.

molecule The smallest unit of a substance that can exist on its own. A molecule consists of one or more atoms held together by chemical forces.

mucus A thick, sticky liquid produced by the lining of some parts of the body.

nasopharynx The tube running from the back of the nose into the back of the mouth.

nitrogen A gas that makes up about four-fifths of the air.

oxygen A gas in the air that we need in order to get energy from food.

pleura A membrane that covers the outside of the lungs and the inside of the ribs.

protein A complex substance made by living things that is used for making some parts of the body and for speeding up the chemical reactions that happen in a cell.

red blood cells The cells that make up most of the blood and carry oxygen around the body.

tissue A part of the body made from cells that are all similar. Muscles are one kind of tissue, and skin is another.

trachea The tube running from the back of the mouth to the lungs. It is also known as the windpipe.

virus A very tiny particle that can infect the cells of living things and cause disease.

white blood cells Several kinds of larger blood cell that are important for defending the body against disease.

Additional resources

Books

Ballard, Carol. *Body Focus: Lungs: Injury, Illness, and Health*. Chicago: Heinemann Library, 2003.

Ballard, Carol. *Exploring the Human Body: The Lungs and Respiration.* San Diego, CA: KidHaven Press, 2005.

Kittredge, Mary. *The Respiratory System.* New York: Chelsea House, 1989.

Walker, Richard. *Encyclopedia of the Human Body*. New York: DK Publishing, 2002.

Web sites

http://www.bbc.co.uk/science/humanbody/
BBC Human Body and Mind: an interactive Web site about the body. The organs section contains information on the lungs and breathing.

http://www.crd.ge.com/esl/cgsp/projects/medical/
A short video flying through the lungs, built up from a series of x-ray scans of the chest.

http://www.enchantedlearning.com/subjects/anatomy/titlepage.shtml
A series of diagrams of different parts of the human anatomy to print out and label.